W9-AJT-173

E
Cou   Counting

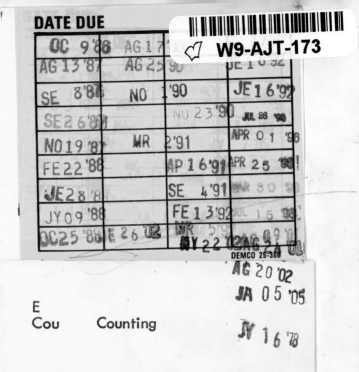

LEARN WITH

E.T.™

COUNTING

Illustrated by Jody Wheeler

Published by Little Simon
Simon & Schuster, New York

Published by LITTLE SIMON, a Simon & Schuster Division of Gulf & Western Corporation.
Simon & Schuster Building, 1230 Avenue of the Americas, New York, New York 10020.
ISBN 0-671-46440-X

76778

1
one lonely Extra-Terrestrial

2

two new friends

3
three bunny rabbits

4

four extra-terrestrial fingers

5
five flower pots

6
six fish in a bowl

7
seven freed frogs

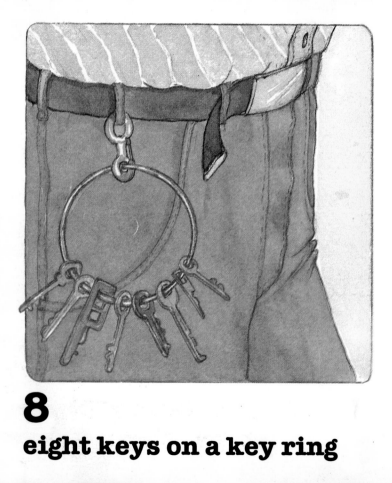

8
eight keys on a key ring

9

**nine children waiting
for a school bus**

10
ten scary masks

11

eleven shining jack-o-lanterns

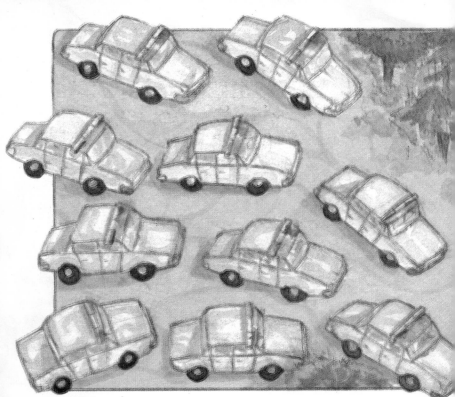

12
twelve police cars in pursuit

13
thirteen tall trees

14
fourteen

strange-looking mushrooms

15
fifteen shining lights

1 **2** **3**

6 **7**

10

12

13

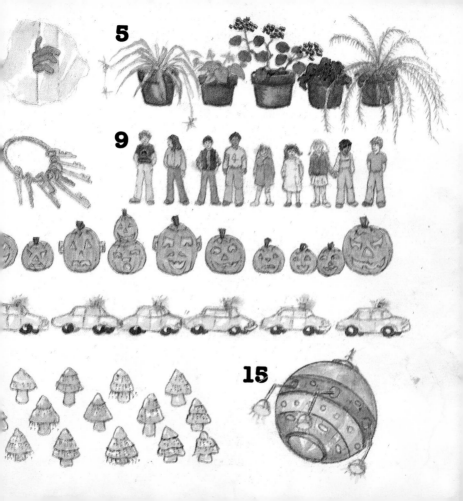

5

9

15

3,000,000

**E.T.'s home: 3 million
light years away**